Simply...
Self-Publishing

Celeste Cuffie

This book is designed to provide inspiration and motivation to our readers through the author's experiences. It is sold with the understanding that the publisher nor author is engaged to render any psychological, legal, or any other kind of professional advice. The content is the sole expression and opinion of its author and not necessarily that of the publisher. Neither the publisher nor the author shall have liability nor responsibility to any person or entity with respect to any loss or damage caused, or alleged to have been caused directly or indirectly by the information contained in this book.

Simply...Self-Publishing

Celeste Cuffie

ISBN-13: 978-1517596927
ISBN-10: 1517596920

www.celestecuffie.com
Twitter-@Celesteempowers
Published By Life Empowered Consulting Services
414 939 LECS

Author's Photograph – Quinn's Photography

DEDICATION

Just in case there is anyone out there who thinks
they can't do it.
Just in case there is anyone who feels that they are
incapable of doing it.
Just in case there is anyone out there who just
doesn't know how to do it.
Just in case there is anyone out there who feels as
though they have to do it alone.
Just in case you are none of the above.
I dedicate this book to you!
Every day that you live, you are being published!
This book is dedicate to all of the publishers of the
world. Those who are publishers by ink and those
publishers by life.

SIMPLY...SELF-PUBLISHING

ACKNOWLEDGMENTS

I want to take a moment to acknowledge all of you who push me outside of my box through your love, support and expectation! To all of those who cheer me on. To all of the future publishers! To all of the past publishers.

IN MEMORY OF

Tom Stevens
Rose Stevens
Jonathan Cuffie
Florida Sheppard
Tina Cowan Wynn

CONTENTS

1 SHARING YOUR STORY

Welcome to the opportunity to share your story, tell a story, or help with someone else's story. When doing either of the three items mentioned, please understand that this undertaking can be both exhilarating and exhausting at the very same time. However, you can do it. Not only can you do it, but there are many ways in which to do it. This book will not cover all of the ways, however we will cover some of the major ones.

Before we get in to the different mediums of

sharing a story, there are some primary questions that you have to ask yourself.

1) Why are you writing?

2) What do you get out of it?

3) What do you want others to get out of it?

4) How important is this project to you?

Understanding and answering these questions will help you to determine the time frame in which it will take you to write and publish your story, the budget that you will allocate for telling your story, and the resources that you will use for your story. So let's begin with those three items.

Whenever you complete any project you will need to consider three items, time, scope, and money. Think of writing a book, like any project such as getting a new car. In order to do that, you need to have the scope or understanding of what the key features of the vehicle are. You will need the money or credit to purchase the new car. You will also need the time to do the adequate research to make sure you are getting a quality vehicle. Now how much you need of each is dependent on how much time you want to spend looking for a car, how much money you are willing to spend on a car, and the features of the car. In this example, if you don't have a lot of time, then you may purchase a car with less features. Conversely, if you don't have a lot of money, you may spend more time researching the vehicle, and leveraging resources to provide your insight on the type of vehicle you are interested in.

I am sure you get my point. So writing a book is much like that, it is leveraging the time, scope, and money in such a way that works best for you as the author.

In this book, we are going to focus on the perspective that you have the time, resources, and money, however you are choosing to publish the book only using your very own blood, sweat, and tears, which is very honorable. Although the principles taught in this book can be used for any genre, I will be using as a consistent example that you are writing an inspirational book about your life. In other words, you are telling your story.

2 PROS AND CONS OF SELF PUBLISHING

So as I just alluded, writing your own book can be as time consuming, draining and as stressful as you allow it to be. Especially if you are placing yourself on a tight time frame and a high expectation to deliver perfection at first completion. Conversely, it can be the most relaxing, healing, and enjoyable experience if you let it. In this chapter, we are going to cover both the pros and the cons of self-publishing.

Let's start with the pros:

1) **Control** – The book is yours from beginning to end. You write the content, you proofread, you choose the book cover design, you do the editing, you do it all. This is control in the highest sense of the word and as a self- publisher you have it.

2) **Profit** - Outside of the costs to print the book, all of the profit is yours. So you have no overhead, just printing costs.

3) **Time** - When trying to get a large publisher to pick up your book, it may take quite a bit of time from when you submit the manuscript, get it approved by the company, and then work on the actual publication of it. As a self-publisher, you are able to set your own deadlines and as long as you adhere to them, your book can be published as soon as you would like.

4) **Satisfaction of completing it on your own** - While this may be overrated to some, there is self - gratification in being able to say that you did it on your own. That you

wrote and published your own book.

Now that we have a good handle on all of the pros and benefits of self-publishing a book let's now talk about some of the cons.

1) **Control** - While there is something to be said about having total control regarding your book and it truly can be a beautiful thing, it can also be a nightmare. This is an area that you honestly have to be transparent with yourself about your strengths and your weaknesses. If you are not the best at having attention to detail, then you should reconsider self-publishing. If sentence structure and formatting feels like a chore for you, then you should reconsider self-publishing. Yielding that control to others may be a necessary evil. It may be uncomfortable and it may also be scary because you are essentially placing your story in someone else's hand. So the con is that you lose control.

2) **Profit** – When you do not self-publish, your profit will have to be shared with your

publisher. The average amount that goes to the publisher is about 25-35%. This is 25-35% less than what you as the author can place in your pocket.

3) **Time** - The time that it may take to write, then review, then to build the cover, then to socialize, can be much longer than expected. Especially if you have to juggle life while working on this project.

4) **Leveraging Publishing Experts** - There are some who get a large amount of satisfaction by doing things on their own. However, you may lose the opportunity to connect with experts who can take your work of art and help make it a masterpiece. So the con in self-publishing is that you give up the ability to leverage the experience that experts can provide.

So we have just discussed the pros and cons of self-publishing. I want to sort of end this chapter with saying that there is a hybrid approach that you can also leverage that will help you get the best of both worlds. I recommend the approach in which you utilize a self-publishing company that also offers services that will meet your needs based on you and your book. So as you continue to go forward, you will find resources that can also be leveraged to help support you in your self-publishing journey. By the end of this book, I am confident that you will be saying "I can publish a book!"

You will also be saying "I will publish MY book."

3 HOW TO WRITE YOUR STORY

Many people talk about writing books, yet they fail to do so. One of the most common obstacles that I hear regarding writing a book is how to start it. So in this section, I am going to tell you just that – how to write your story.

When speaking to the hundreds of people that I have about writing a book, the conversation usually begins and ends around the process of writing. I often walk away with the perspective that people think that they should be able to just sit down and write a perfect, cohesive, organized, and succinct story in just one sitting. That means that all of the commas are in the correct place, all of the sentences grammatically correct, and that all of the chapters flow as smoothly as melted chocolate. However, that's a fallacy. I will share with you in Chapter 4 what you should be doing after you have "completed" (notice the quotes) your book.

Follow these simple steps to successfully write your story.

1) **Commit a certain time to spend on writing.** Meaning, commit to 2 hours a week or 4 hours a month, whatever that is for you, commit to it.

2) **Find your space that will inspire you to write.** So now you are ready to spend some time writing, and let's say you are writing about events that took place while you were a child. Last month, for your committed time, you sat and wrote in the

coffee shop, near the home you grew up in. This month you may be writing in your home office with nostalgic music playing and old photos spread out on your desk. Whatever you have to do in order to make writing conducive for you, don't be afraid to do it.

3) **Just write.** Initially, don't worry about formatting, flow, organization, chapter titles, number of pages, none of that yet. Just write. Get whatever your story is on paper and then worry about the details. If this is too unstructured for you, then create a high level outline. That means write a subject or goal of each section (don't term it a chapter yet) that you plan to write. However do not hesitate to add or remove sections when you deem it necessary. Remember this is YOUR book, you get to write it your way.

4) **Find value in your own story.** When working to honor your commitment in

writing your story, you may get discouraged, tired, or simply unmotivated. Think about what the result of telling your story will do. Go back to the initial questions of why you are writing, allow your answers to be the motivation needed to get you writing again.

5) **Find fun.** In your writing you may be sharing some difficult topics. However, when it gets heavy don't hesitate to jump subjects and write a fun or happy story that you can recall. Then go back later to the more difficult one.

6) **Find yourself a publishing partner.** Tell someone that you trust that you are writing a book. Ask this person to encourage you, support you, and push you to get your book published.

Notice that it wasn't until item six that getting the book published was even acknowledged. That's because before you can publish a book, you have to write it. And there's no need to edit or discuss publishing what isn't even on paper yet. Just get everything down that you think you want to share. Then build from there. Following the above indicated six steps will get you a very strong first draft completed in no time (that is if you honored your time commitment to yourself). So now that you have that completed, walk away for 14 days.

Taking 14 days off from your book will allow you to come back and review it with fresh eyes. The details of editing, organizing, and overall cleanup can be overwhelming but this book will help you relieve some of the pressures. Using your fresh eyes, you will see themes, and trends which will help you reorganize and edit much easier.

During this time off, don't even think about the book. Celebrate the completion of your first milestone. Relish in the fact that you have written a book. Regardless to it being published or not, you have told the story that you wanted to tell and that is worthy of celebration.

4 HOW TO EDIT YOUR STORY

You have taken time away from the book, you have rested your mind, and you have celebrated the fact that you have completed the book. Now you are back and ready. You are ready to review your book with fresh eyes and fresh insight. Your book should be reviewed with fresh eyes. Your next steps are to review, reevaluate, rearrange, and revisit.

There are several strategies to assess a book, but my strong recommendation is that you leverage the old fashioned way. Grab you a highlighter, colored ink pen, book, and a blank piece of paper.

PRINT OUT your book with page numbers!

Yes, print it out. No matter how many pages it is, invest in you.

1) **Review** - Take your draft and read it from beginning to end.

2) **Reevaluate** - Identify if there are things that you want to add or remove from the book. Always keep in mind that when you write a book, anyone (and I mean anyone) in the world has the potential to read your story. So if there is something that you are not ready to share, reconsider including it in your book. Conversely, as you are reading your book, you may also remember something else that you may want to add to the story. Do not hesitate to expand.

So here is how you do it:

If you are removing something - Simply take your colored ink pen and cross it out.

If you are adding something - Highlight the area that you want to place it in. Put a letter next to that section. Then grab a blank piece of paper, write the page number and the letter that you indicated for that section, and then write what you would like to add.

When you get back to your computer, you will have corresponding letters and pages for your updates.

3) **Rearrange** - As you are reviewing and reevaluating, you may also want to take items and move them around. You may see some trends or some things that may be better suited in another part of the book. This is your opportunity for you to do that.

For example, if you are reviewing page 72 of your

book and now believe the story about your pet Skippy is better suited on page 35, then highlight the story on page 72 and make a note in the margin to say move to page 35. Then go to page 35 and draw a line indicating where you want the story to go and make a note in the margin saying add story from page 72. If you have multiple items moving, then add the alphabet convention.

This is the overall process for editing your book. I also want to make mention of some tips as you are preparing to publish your book.

- ☐ It's your story, you get to tell it your way! If you want to tell your story from your perspective, you get to do that. It's yours.
- ☐ When you see errors, and items not grammatically correct (such as slang), you may have decided to do that on purpose and that is ok. Just be consistent.
- ☐ Be aware of margins. Since books are not perfectly flat, I encourage you to use wider margins on the inside of the book where the binding or bridge is located.

- ☐ Leverage any resources that you can. Have your publishing partner review and critique. Consider using some of the resources from your selected publishing company.
- ☐ Read it backwards. I am still not sure why this works, but it does.
- ☐ Don't rush to finish the book and use your time breaks, they are critical.

4) **Revisit** - As you are going through the review, reevaluate, and rearrange stages, this is where you will also begin to clean up your chapters while you are organizing. Once you feel pretty good about where you are, put it down again. Wait 14 days then revisit. Start the process all over again. About four iterations with the 14 day breaks in between. When you think you are near perfect, wait 30 days, then pick it back up.

5 PUBLISH YOUR STORY

Now for the good stuff. There are several self-publishing sites that you can leverage to help you publish your book. You can be completely self-published meaning that you wrote the book, go through the technicalities of your ISBN number, creating a cover and deciding if your book will be a paper book, e-book or both. From there, you place your order and then you're done! You have done the entire book on your own, only leveraging the publishing company to print the book. The other option would be to leverage the services that your publishing company has and allow them to support you in the process (for a fee of course). Remember, there is time, scope, and money. It is very likely that you will have a good amount of two of the three items, and you get to choose which two.

A few self-publishing websites to consider are Createspace, Outskirts Press, and Lulu. While there are several more out there, these are a great starting point.

When you are deciding on a company, some items to consider are:

1) **Company's capability** - Can the company provide you with all that you need. What is their level of customer service? What additional services do they offer? Is there something that you may need that the company does not offer? What about someone to do the final review?

2) **Cost** – Does the cost seem reasonable for what you are looking to do? What are the services included in the cost? What are the royalties? The average royalties

are about 40%, for self-published books, so how many books will you have to sell to get a return on your investment?

3) **Timeliness** – Should you decide to create a paper copy of your book, how long will it take for the book to arrive?

4) **Exposure** – Where will your books be available for purchase at? Will you be able to purchase them on the Barnes and Noble website as well as Amazon? Where else?

6 YOU CAN DO IT!

You have gotten to the near conclusion of the book, and with all of the tools and information handy you simply have to make up your mind to do it! Once you decide to do it, you can and will do it. I am your publishing partner, cheering you on. I'm here just to let you know that you can do anything that you put your mind to. So go for it! Take a deep breath and press the button to order your books!

Congratulations! You have completed the due diligence of writing your story. You have put on paper your story. You have leveraged your publishing partner to help you get it done. You have now went through the process of reviewing, reevaluating, rearranging, and revisiting your book, all while allowing time to be your friend. You have honored your commitment to yourself and as a result, you are just steps away from your goal. You have done your research and have picked a site to publish your book, you have submitted your book, created your cover and now you just have to wait. Patiently wait for your very first order of books that will contain your story, the one that you want to share with the world that will help them during this journey called life.

Common Types of Publications:

Paper book
Ebook
Audio book

Popular Self-Publishers

Xlibris
Createspace
Diggypod
LuLu
Infinity Publishing

QUICK ORDER FORM

Simply... Self-Publishing

List Price $6.95

Website: www.celestecuffie.com

Telephone Orders Call 1414.939.LECS

For speaking engagements, seminars, or interviews, call or email requests to the information listed above.